"These poems come from Haunani-Kay Trask, who lives in Hawai'i but writes for all who live in the Africas, the Americas, Asia, Europe, and Polynesia—wherever people have been colonized or dispossessed. She does not simply write with a pen; she slashes with it. She is truly a gift from the Gods."—Witi Ihimaera

"*Night Is a Sharkskin Drum* is the only book that I've read through at least six times—and with increasing interest and appreciation each time. I love it. It's that good." —Epeli Hau'ofa

Night Is a Sharkskin Drum

Talanoa: Contemporary Pacific Literature

NIGHT IS A SHARKSKIN DRUM

Haunani-Kay Trask

Talanoa: Contemporary Pacific Literature
University of Hawai'i Press
Honolulu

Printed in the United States of America

02   03   04   05   06   07   6   5   4   3   2   1

Library of Congress Cataloging-in-Publication Data
Trask, Haunani-Kay.
Night is a sharkskin drum / Haunani-Kay Trask.
p.   cm.
ISBN 0–8248–2616–7 (hardcover : alk. paper) —
ISBN 0–8248–2570–5 (pbk. : alk. paper)
1. Hawaii—poetry.   I. Title.
PS3570.R3374   N54   2002
811'.54—dc21
2002001545

University of Hawai'i Press books are printed on acid-free
paper and meet the guidelines for permanence and
durability of the Council on Library Resources.

Designed by Carol Colbath

Printed by Edwards Brothers

For Ngũgĩ

CONTENTS

ACKNOWLEDGMENTS

The poems "Smiling Corpses," "Sovereignty," and "Together" are anthologized in *Wasafiri* no. 25 (spring 1997). The poems "The Broken Gourd" and "Nāmakaokahaʻi" are anthologized in *Social Process in Hawaiʻi* 38 (1997). The poems "Before Dawn Leaves Forever," "Born in Fire," "Hiʻiaka Chanting," "Kona Kaiʻōpua," "Lahaina, 1995," "The Mist of My Heart," "Nāmahakokahaʻi," "Night Is a Sharkskin Drum," "Pūowaina: Flag Day," "Returning," "Smiling Corpses," "Tourist," and "Who Would Find the Midnight Rainbow" are anthologized in *Anglistica* 2, no. 1 (1998). The poems "Born in Fire," "Hiʻiaka Chanting," "Nāmakaokahaʻi," "Night Is a Sharkskin Drum," and "Who Would Find the Midnight Rainbow" are anthologized in *ʻŌiwi: A Native Hawaiian Journal* (December 1998). The poems "Dispossessions of Empire," "Lahaina, 1995," "Nāmakaokahaʻi," "Pūowaina: Flag Day," and "Smiling Corpses" are anthologized in *Inside Out: Literature, Cultural Politics, and Identity in the New Pacific,* ed. Vilsoni Hereniko and Rob Wilson (Philadelphia: Rowman & Littlefield, 1999). The poems "Afternoons," "The Shallows," "Sweeten the Mango," "Open Your Weariness," "To Write by Moonlight," and "Where the Fern Clings," are anthologized in Haunani-Kay Trask, *Light in the Crevice Never Seen,* revised edition, (Corvallis, Ore.: Calyx Books, 1999). The poems "Lahaina, 1995" and "Tourist" are anthologized in *Literary Studies East and West* 17 (2000). The poem "Into Our Light I Will Go Forever" is anthologized in *Rampike* 11, no. 2 (2000). The poems "The Flute of the *ʻOhe,*" "Kona Kaiʻōpua," and "Ruins" are anthologized in *ʻŌiwi: A Native Hawaiian Journal,* July 2002.

I

Born in Fire

Born in Fire

Born in fire
    you came through
        the mountainous dead

    to find sandalwood
        forests, skeins of fern
            the plump *pulu*
                of the *hāpuʻu.*

    Flickering *lehua*
        guided you here.
            Stay, now, within

            the trembling breast
                of Pele, steaming her
                    breath into the trees

    drawing your fires
        to her craterous womb

        consuming your passionate heat.

Who Would Find the Midnight Rainbow

for Damien

who would find the midnight
  rainbow, *lei* of Pana'ewa?

    who would follow
      Hōpoe's forest,
        shimmering with Hina?

    who would seek the woman
      of Kīlauea, smoldering
        in her caldera?

    who would *oli*
      in the bosom of Pele
        wreathed in flame?

Night Is a Sharkskin Drum

Night is a sharkskin drum
      sounding our bodies black
         and gold.

        All is aflame
     the uplands a *shush*
          of wind.

        From Halemaʻumaʻu
          our fiery Akua comes:

E, Pele *e*,

       E, Pele *e*,

              E, Pele *e*.

Hiʻiaka Chanting

Glistening tree snails
    miraculous light gleaming
       ʻōlapa leaves

    in Pele's uplands.
        Elegant *hāpuʻu*, translucent
          as her eyes. And

      our flitting *iʻiwi*
        nimble beak sipping
         love's *lehua*

      buds. Winter moss
        sponging the earth. Hypnotic
         mist. Hiʻiaka chanting

      on the wind.
        Step lightly, dancer.
         Look up, look up.

Nāmakaokahaʻi

Born from the chest
   of Haumea, *moʻo*
      woman of *kuapā,*
   lizard-tongued goddess
      of Hawaiʻi:
         Nāmakaokahaʻi,
            sister of thunder
   and shark—
      Kānehekili,
         Kūhaimoana—
   elder of Pele,
      Pelehonuamea.

Kino lau on the wind,
         in the yellowing *ti,*
            sounds of Akua
               awaking in the dawn:

      Nā-maka-o-ka-haʻi,
         eyes flecked with fire,
            summoning her family

        from across the seas.

Sharks in the shallows,
      upheaval in the heavens.

From the red rising mist
              of Kahiki, the Woman of the Pit:

Pele, Pele'aihonua,
              traveling the uplands,

devouring the foreigner.

II

A Fragrance of Devouring

The Broken Gourd

After the last echo
where fingers of light
soft as *laua'e*
come slowly

toward our aching earth,
a cracked *ipu*
whispers, bloody water
on its broken lip.

Long ago, wise *kānaka*
hauled hand-twined
nets, whole villages shouting
the black flash of fish.

Wāhine u'i
trained to the chant
of roiling surf;
nā keiki sprouted by the sun
of a blazing sky.

Even Hina, tinted
by love, shone gold
across a lover's sea.

11

This night I crawl
into the mossy arms
of upland winds,

an island's moan
welling grief:

Each of us slain
by the white claw
of history: lost
genealogies, propertied
missionaries, diseased
haole.

Now, a poisoned *pae ʻāina*
swarming with foreigners

and dying Hawaiians.

III.

A common horizon:
smelly shores
under spidery moons,

pockmarked *maile* vines,
rotting *'ulu* groves,
the brittle *clack*
of broken lava stones.

Out of the east
a damp stench of money
burning at the edges.

Out of the west
the din of divine
violence, triumphal
destruction.

At home, the bladed
reverberations of empire.

Ruins

To choose the late noon
  sun, running barefoot
    on wet Waimānalo
      beach; to go with all

    our souls' lost yearnings
      to that deeper place
        where love has let
          the stars come down

      and my hair, shawled
        over bare shoulders,
          falls in black waves
        across my face;

  there, at last,
    escaped from the ruins
      of our nation,

        to lift our voices
          over the sea
            in bitter songs
              of mourning.

The Flute of the 'Ohe

The flute of the *'ohe*
    filters our music:
        notes of the burning
           the jeweled, the tender
           dead.

    Here, in our wanderings,
        disembodied islands
           turn yellow, rotting
                in a human forest.

        Over the ancient roads,
           muddy waters are
                rushing, ant-hills
                    moving inland,
           the twilight horizon closing.

In the anguished
    hours, loud-voiced foreigners
        ravage the land at will.

Kona Kaiʻōpua

Across a fathomless horizon,
    koa voyaging canoes

        plumed Kanaloa,
            provocative summer clouds

            gilded by the god:
        blue pearl, green
    olivine. In the Kona

noon, a lone *naiʻa*—
    sea-sleek *kino lau*
        of divinity.

        Between coastal *heiau*
            castrated *niu,* shorn

    of fruit and flower,
        fawning. From the ancestral
        shore, *tlack-tlack*

    of lava stones, massaged
        by tidal seas: eternal
        kanikau for long-

forgotten *ali'i*, entombed
beneath grandiose hotels
mocked

by crass amusements
Japanese machines
and the common greed

of vulgar Americans.

Lahaina, 1995

This is not Marti's Cuba.
    No warriors await
        the call to freedom's

        arms. Here, drifting trash
            clogs the shores, coating
                the lost minds

                    of burnt-red tourists
    staining the sand
        with acrid oils.

        The natives don't
            horde small fortunes
                for revolution's
                    duty. They sit,

   observing the parade, or
        jump to join the passing

fleet of noisy cars,
        waving at their destiny
            a musical good-bye,

                suffused with a sweet
                    intention to smile

        and be happy.

Tourist

The flourishing hand
 of greed, a predatory

  face without dreams.
   In the marketplace,

    glittering knives of money,
    murdering the trees.

Nostalgia: VJ-Day

I.

A wounded morning
   crippled by helicopters.
      No bulletproof skies
         over our "Hawaiian Islands"

      where presidents and
         enemies dismember
            this charmed Pacific.
               Now, the exalted 50th

         anniversary of VJ-Day.[1]
            Parade of the ancients: marines,
               G.I.'s, the all-Filipino
                  regiment reminiscing

         in faded uniform,
            feted by a Commander-
               in-Chief ascending on bursts
                  of rhetoric, but deftly

avoiding Vietnam, the wrong
   war, inglorious
      embarrassment.
         And there, our authentic

Japanese senator, smugly
            armless from the great war,
                preposterous manikin
                    of empire, feigning an
                        accent (American East

coast or late British
            colonial) proving
                acculturation by
                    perfect imitation.[2]

II.

At the grave sites, tens
            of thousands of tourists;
                National Cemetery
                    of the Pacific: honoring

war dead by waving
            American flags
                in a faraway land.
                    Red, white, and blue,

Old Glory, old glory.
        At Waikīkī and Pearl
            Harbor, maneuvers
                and air shows: jets,

carriers, even a black
    "stealth bomber," modeled
        by *Star Trek*. Ah!
            the long-ago days

of real war, remembered
    with tears, when killing
        was simple, and tall,
            young warriors went down

to bloodless death
    in the noblest reaches
        of empire: the United
            States of America.

Notes

1. VJ-Day in Hawai'i commemorates victory over Japan in the Second World War.

2. The Japanese senator, who is "smugly armless from the great war," refers to Daniel Inouye, senior U.S. senator from Hawai'i. He lost his arm in the Second World War and has refused to use a prosthesis ever since, choosing to parade his empty sleeve as a sign of his patriotism to the United States of America.

Smiling Corpses

Smiling corpses
　　　　of the Democratic Party

　　　wander through an undulating
　　　　sea of money, thin waves
　　　　　　of lethargic green.

　　　Moist statues rise up
　　　　wipe their lidded eyes
　　　　　　begin stalking.

　　　　In the sky, broken clouds
　　　　　crawl off the sun.

Below, from the banana spires,
　　　　rotten steam,

　　　　　a fragrance
　　　　　　of devouring.

Sovereignty

No shadow falls across
those volcanic labia
of fern and spongy
cliff, flooded
by the sun
of revelation.

Nā *wahi pana*:
the sacred places.

At midday
gargantuan blades
dismember our peace:
twin-engine Americans,
amphibious marine
assassins.

II.

Aztecs called winsome
Montezuma "the whore
of the Spanish," bringer
of betrayal.

Before the conquerors
could finish their duty
all the children
lay dying
from the pox
or the sword;

all the women
lay silent, mouths
stuffed with their own
breasts; all the men
had fallen, in pieces,
to savage hounds.

III.

Now, our own Montezuma
goes pandering: Waiheʻe,
"runny squid water"

slithering across
the land, slime and
pestilence in his wake.
Plunder

and monstrosities:
snaking freeways,
Japanese resorts,
the fester of Native favelas:

Kalihi, Wai'anae
Mākaha.

IV.

After the noise
of commemoration,
helicopters and jets:

metal raptors
come to feast
on our dead.

In 1993, poisoned islands
the stench of treason:

Waihe'e, Kamali'i,
Kamau'u, Akaka.
"Hawaiians" promising
deliverance

with the whine
of betrayal.

Pūowaina: Flag Day

for Ka'iana, Lākea, Mililani, Hulali, and Kalai'ola'a

Bring ginger, yellow
and white, broken stalks
with glossy leaves.

        Bring *lei hulu,*
        palapalai, pīkake. Bring
        kapa, beaten fine

                as skin. Bring
                the children
                to chant

                        for our dead,
                        then stand
                        with the *lāhui*

                        and burn
                        their American
                        flag.

Nā ʻŌiwi

I.

How is it
    your black Hawaiian hair,
        flowing in red-tipped waves,
            a cloak of fine, burnt feathers

from our ancient past,
    now rests on white
        coffin folds, false satin
            finish in the gloss,

as if our people couldn't
    tell by their touch
        the undertaker's hand, as if
            the gleam of your magnificent

time could be muted
    by the waxy smell
        of missionary lies.

II.

How is it now
     you are gone,
          our *ali'i* dismembered,
               their *mana* lost,

we are left
     with broken bodies, blinded
          children, infected winds
               from across the sea.

How is it,
     our bones cry out
          in their infinite dying,
               the *haole* and their ways

               have come to stay.

At Punaluʻu

Every tourist, a camera
            to capture us Natives;
    the slant of their lens
            diminishing Hawaiians.

    Japan Japanese just from
            Tokyo; Hong Kong Chinese
    and tall Taiwanese,
            Asia's dragons

                stumbling over lava,
    misfits in Guccis
            and matching hats,
    frightened by waves and jet-

            black sand. Near trinket
                    stalls, a Nikon moment:
    hawksbill turtles and
            sundark surfers.

Triumph of the will:
        endangered species
     frozen on film,
        Native images

          for millions back
        home: "Paradise
           at Punaluʻu: Made
              in Japan."

Dispossessions of Empire

I.

Aku boats lazing
   on the aqua horizon
waves of morning, a seawind
   sun, salt hanging

   in the steamy Kona
      glare, lava-black shore
   rippling along rocky
      outcrops, porous with *loli.*

      Slow-footed Hawaiians
         amidst flaunting
      foreigners: rich
         Americans, richer

      Japanese, smelling
         of greasy perfume,
      tanning with the stench
         of empire.

II.

Escape: the currency
    of travel, lure
        of colonies. How strange
            the strangers'

ways. White-skinned
    hominids burning pink
        against indigenous brown,
            traveling the blessed

isles in aimless journeys.
    Fecund, the offerings
        of mysterious Polynesians:
            "bejeweled Kaua'i,"

"majestic Maui,"
    "volcanic Hawai'i . . ."
        "The Hawaiian Islands," one off
            the tourist log of fun.

III.

Even prostitutes know
their profession, but natives?

The empire degrades
through monetary exchange,
leaving quaint Hawaiians
dressing as "natives,"

in drag for the 10 o'clock
floor show, faking
a singsong pidgin
with the drunken crowd

hoping for tips
after the French kisses.

. . . nothing amiss
in the morass of Paradise.

IV.

An orphaned smell
of ghettos in this tourist
archipelago: shanties
on the beach, slums

in the valleys, corruption
        and trash everywhere.
In the city, immigrants
        claiming to be natives;

        in the country, natives
without a nation:
        The democracy of colonies.

                For the foreigner, romances
                        of "Aloha,"
                For Hawaiians,
                        dispossessions of empire.

III

CHANTS OF DAWN

Still Is the Fern

Still is the fern,
      hāpuʻu and *palaʻā*

Cool, the footfall
      of Hiʻiaka.

          In burning snow,
          slumbering Mauna Kea.

              Arise and go,
              sacred, into dawn.

To Hear the Mornings

To hear the mornings
    among *hāpuʻu:* a purity
of cardinals, cunning bees
    in shell-covered sleeves
       of honeysuckle,
          . . . the aqua undertones
       of cooing doves.

To seek our scarlet
    ʻapapane, Hōpoe restless
       amongst the *liko*
         and *ʻōlapa* trees,
       shimmering the leaves,
         . . . *shush-shush*
           of burnt rain
              sweeping in from Puna.

To watch our lustrous
    volcanic dawn seducing
       ʻelepaio, speckled beak
    sucking *ʻōhelo* berries
       oozing sap
         under a crimson sun.

To breathe the Akua:
    lehua and *makani*,
      pua and *lāʻī*,
        maile and *palai*,
          . . . pungent *kino lau*.

To sense the ancients,
      ka wā mamua—from time before
   slumbering still
     amidst the forests
       of Kaʻū, within the bosom
       of Pele.

To honor and chant,
   by the sound
     of the *pū*, our
   ageless genealogy:
ʻāina aloha,
   ʻāina hānau,
     . . . this generous, native Hawaiʻi.

Returning

for Michael

Honi of rain and cloud
        dawn light,

blue movement. *Ti, ʻulu, maiʻa*

      steaming. Sweetfern
             Koʻolau, chiseled by sun

        humming undersongs:
         ʻohe, maile, tiare.

Slow-hipped Kāneʻohe,
        wet-scented lover

        chanting
           us in.

"Shipwrecked on the Shallows of the Stars"

—Odysseus Elytis

I.

I lie awake
    at the edge of clouds

        a rustling shore
            embraced by winds.

Into the mountains
    the shells and I

        fevered with moon.

Below, giant mollusks

           in a floating dusk.

II.

On the breast of the rain
a passionate sea

longing for flight

and the voyaging sun
in coral waters beyond.

My spangled hair
wanders toward light:

a sudden waterfall
of stars.

From Kaʻaʻawa to Rarotonga

rainswept banana groves
   under a burdened sky

    refreshed by smells
      of seawind, blowing

       clouds to breadfruit islands,
         my tribal spirit

           dreaming flight,
             from Kaʻaʻawa
               to Rarotonga

                   high-soaring *ʻiwa*
                     plying the Pacific
                       with Maui's hook

Afternoons

afternoons glisten
with innocence, the flowering
heart a serene evening
ingathered by the wind

at midnight my burning lips
recall a song of fountains
soft flame and veil
for a voice of oiled leaves

through tangled grasses
the scent of men: breadfruit
and banana

in the fevered dawn
of gods

Where Is the Elegant Light

where is the elegant
        light, intimate
                finger of lovers?

                where is the breast
                        of sea, tender
                                dark perfection?

                where is the crevice
                        of rose, pleasure's
                                infinite sun?

                                where is woman's
                                        desire, moonlit
                                                eternity?

Upon the Dark of Passion

Upon the dark of passion
    lay gardenias, soundless

as moonlight. Let our shadows
    swell into longing

between breadfruit
    and palm, throbbing

in the leaves.
    Cast into rings

the echo of our bodies,
    scented and burning

        darker in our arms.

Where the Fern Clings

where the fern
clings, lingering
above slit

     rock, shadows
     musky in hot
     perfume

          . . . the cries
          of tight-winged birds

               flickering tongues,
                  damplit skin,

                    the seep
                        of summer
                            thirst

To Write by Moonlight

To write by moonlight,

    mai'a leaves, the green
        ink of night;

        silvered *niu,*
            the hair of dark's

            blue quill. To weave
                our moist, reedy fog

                through Hina's
                    estuary; gleam

    and shade cool
        hunehune winds.

            To yield a tart
                earthen slime
                    of ripe mango;

    tint the ocean's
        prism with burnt
            kamani gold,

then gaze
    at dawn's
        lush diffusion

      and chant before
          our vaulting Koʻolau.

The Shallows

Your sea-blue
 eyes, the shallows

  and reef
   of Waimānalo

an underwater
 morning
  of caves

  filled with
   cooled lava

   and little
    sparkling fish.

The Mist of My Heart

The mist of my heart
    travels to Waimānalo,

    embracing there
        the salt of the sea.

        Two *koaʻe* birds
            entwine their long tails

                secretly.

He'eia Uli

Risen from the waters
of Waimānalo, across

the eyes of Olomana,
down the scrotum

of Kōnāhuanui,
over the thighs

of Ko'olau Poko,
pregnant Hina

arrives. In the cool
of He'eia Uli,

bathing her breasts,
she gleams,

remembering
Pō Mahina.

Run into the Sea

for Pi'ikea

Run into the sea,
>   pale foam and plume
>   glittering the green.

>   Dive through
>   Makapu'u's
>   silvery weave,

>   *līpoa* and spume
>   salting the wind.
>   Glide on summer's

>   turquoise luck, black
>   *hīhīmanu*
>   under you.

Sweeten the Mango

Sweeten the mango
        with moonlight,

               lei of gold
                        and longing;

       leaves of cloud
                 incandescent,

          mele of Kāne'ohe
                 calling,
                      calling.

Open Your Weariness

Open your weariness
     wahine of red,

    abandon the road
        of dust and stone.

      Let freedom fly
         to coral islands,

          lithe monk seals,
            and the sting
              of freshest seas.

Before Dawn Leaves Forever

Before dawn leaves forever
        let us embrace
                over half-open horizons
                        rose glinting the tall grasses.

            Above the stars and spilt violet
                let us offer ourselves,
                    again.

                Where the wide surf
                    rolls across islands
                            let us follow, trembling
                                into blue light.

                    Out of the elegies
                        of love, let us enter
                            summer's last sun.

Together

for Mililani

Comrades follow
over the constant waves.

Blue, now gold
a great *honu* follows.

Beyond the leaping
point, our souls
depart.

More beautiful still.

Into Our Light I Will Go Forever

Into our light
    I will go forever.

    Into our seaweed
        clouds and saltwarm
            seabirds.

Into our windswept
   'ehu kai, burnt
      sands gleaming.

    Into our sanctuaries
        of hushed bamboo,
           awash in amber.

  Into the passion
     of our parted Ko'olau,
        luminous vulva.

    Into Kāne's pendulous
      breadfruit, resinous
        with semen.

Into our wetlands
      of Heʻeia,
            bubbling black mud.

Into our spangled,
      blue-leafed *taro,*
           flooded with *wai.*

Into Waiāhole,
      chattering with rains
           and silvered fish.

Into our shallows
      of Kualoa,
           translucent Akua.

Into the hum of
      reef-ringed Kaʻaʻawa,
           pungent with *limu.*

Into our corals of
      far Kahana, sea-cave
           of Hina.

Into our chambered
      springs of Punaluʻu,
           ginger misting.

Into the songs of
　　lost Lāʻie, cool
　　　　light haunting.

Into murmuring
　　Mālaekahana,
　　　　plumed sands chanting.

Into the sheen
　　of flickering Haleʻiwa,
　　　　pearled with salt.

Into the *waʻa* of
　　Kanaloa, voyaging
　　　　moana nui.

Into our sovereign suns,
　　drunk on the *mana*
　　　　of Hawaiʻi.

GLOSSARY

ʻāina	Land, earth
ʻāina aloha	Beloved land
ʻāina hānau	The land of one's birth
aku	Bonito, skipjack tuna
Akua	God; supernatural; divine
aliʻi	Chief
aloha	Love, greeting
ʻapapane	Hawaiian honeycreeper with crimson body and black wings and tail, found on all the main Hawaiian Islands. Its feathers occasionally were used for featherwork.
ʻehu kai	Sea spray, foam
ʻelepaio	A species of flycatcher with subspecies on Hawaiʻi, Kauaʻi, and Oʻahu
Haleʻiwa	Small community on the north shore of Oʻahu; literally, house of frigate birds
Halemaʻumaʻu	Firepit in Kīlauea crater, island of Hawaiʻi; one of the many places where the volcano deity, Pele, lives; literally, ʻamaʻu fern house
haole	Foreign; also, white people
hāpuʻu	Endemic tree fern of the Hawaiian archipelago, found in abundance in forests at Kīlauea volcano
Haumea	Earth mother who, with her husband, Wākea—sky father—created the Hawaiian people

Hawai'i	Largest of the eight major Hawaiian Islands; home of the volcano goddess, Pele
He'eia	Lush land division on the windward, Ko'olau side of the island of O'ahu
He'eia Uli	One of two parts of the He'eia land division; called dark *(uli)* He'eia because it is in the lush, green uplands, as opposed to He'eia Kea—white He'eia—which is near the sea
heiau	Temple of worship. Many temples existed in traditional Hawai'i, including large, elaborate temples for human sacrifice.
hīhīmanu	Various eagle rays and stingrays
Hi'iaka	Deity of the forest on the island of Hawai'i; one of the sisters of Pele
Hina	Goddess, the moon
honi	Kiss; traditional greeting where noses are pressed in affection
honu	Turtle
Hōpoe	Beloved friend of Hi'iaka whose emblem is the flowering *lehua* tree of the island of Hawai'i
hunehune	Fine or delicate, as in fern or mist
i'iwi	Scarlet Hawaiian honeycreeper
ipu	Gourd, drum made from a gourd
'iwa	Frigate bird or man-of-war bird
Ka'a'awa	One of sixteen traditional land divisions *(ahupua'a)* in the Ko'olauloa area of O'ahu
Kahana	A valley, bay, and stream on O'ahu

Kahiki	Tahiti; place where Hawaiians return upon death
Kalihi	Section of Honolulu
kamani	Native hardwood tree that grows near the beach and has large leaves with fall colors
kānaka	The Hawaiian people
Kanaloa	Major Hawaiian male deity of the Pacific Ocean
Kāne	Major Hawaiian male deity of the land. Kāne appeared in many manifestations, including breadfruit and banana.
Kānehekili	God of lightning
Kāneʻohe	Land division on the windward side of Oʻahu known for wetlands, the majestic Koʻolau mountains, and a large, calm bay; literally, the bamboo of the god Kāne; or alternately, bamboo husband
kanikau	Dirge, lamentation, chant of mourning
kapa	Cloth made from pounded bark; clothes
Kaʻū	Land district on the island of Hawaiʻi; literally, the breast
Kauaʻi	One of the eight major Hawaiian Islands, known for its lush beauty
ka wā mamua	"The time before": a reference to ancient times
Kīlauea	Active volcanic crater on the island of Hawaiʻi; said to be the home of Pele, goddess of the volcano

kino lau	Many forms taken by a god, such as the *ti* leaf as a form of the *mo'o* (lizard) god
koa	Large native forest tree, with crescent leaves; fine red wood formerly used for canoes, now for furniture, calabashes, and *'ukulele*
koa'e	The boatswain bird
Kona	Place on the island of Hawai'i; also, the dry, leeward side of any of the Hawaiian Islands
Kōnāhuanui	Peaks above Nu'uanu Pali, O'ahu; literally, his great testicles
Kona Kai'ōpua	Poetic name for Kona. *Kai'ōpua* refers to the billowy clouds above the vast reefless sea of Kona.
Ko'olau	Windward sides of the Hawaiian Islands
Ko'olau Poko	One of the districts of windward O'ahu
Kualoa	Land division, point, and beach park on the windward side of O'ahu considered one of the most sacred places on the island
kuapā	Wall of a fishpond
Kūhaimoana	Largest and most celebrated of Hawaiian shark gods
Lahaina	Place on the island of Maui; once a whaling town, now a popular tourist haven despoiled with trinket shops, hotels, and foreigners
lāhui	People, nation
lā'ī	*Ti* leaf

Lā'ie	Land section and bay on the windward side of O'ahu
laua'e	A fragrant fern
lehua	A bright red fuzzy flower of the '*ōhi'a* tree; also the tree itself; symbol of the island of Hawai'i
lei	A wreath worn around the neck, usually of flowers, leaves, or shells
lei hulu	Feather *lei,* formerly worn by royalty; a beloved child or person
liko	Leaf bud of the '*ōhi'a lehua* tree
limu	General name for all plants living under water, salt or fresh
līpoa	Many-branched edible brown seaweed known for its strong, distinctive smell
loli	Sea cucumber
mai'a	Banana
maile	A native twining shrub with fragrant shiny leaves used for decoration and *lei*
Mākaha	Land division from the mountains to the sea between Wai'anae and Kea'au on O'ahu, famous in modern times for huge winter surf
makani	Wind, breeze
Makapu'u	Rocky point that juts into the ocean at east O'ahu; literally, bulging eye
Mālaekahana	Land division and stream near Kahuku on O'ahu's north shore
mana	Divine power
Maui	Trickster god of Polynesia; also, the second largest island in the Hawaiian chain

Mauna Kea	Massive mountain on Hawai'i Island; literally, white mountain
mele	Song
moana nui	The deep ocean; literally, big sea
mo'o	Lizard; reptile of any kind; water spirit
nai'a	Porpoise
nā keiki	Children
Nāmakaokaha'i	Elder *mo'o* sister of Pele, goddess of the volcano
nā 'ōiwi	The Hawaiian people
nā wahi pana	Sacred places
niu	The coconut palm, a male symbol
'ohe	All kinds of bamboo; flute
'ōhelo	Small native shrub in the cranberry family
'ōlapa	Several native species of forest trees with green leaves that flutter like aspen trees; dancer as contrasted with the chanter; dance accompanied by chanting and drumming on a gourd drum
oli	Chant, especially with prolonged phrases in one breath
Olomana	A beautiful, pointed peak in Kailua named for a noted O'ahu island chief of ancient times
pae'āina	Group of islands, archipelago
pala'ā	The common lace fern, wild in Hawai'i
palai	Native Hawaiian fern, important to Laka, goddess of the *hula*, i.e., of Hawaiian dance
palapalai	Different types of native fern, ranging in height from one to four feet

Pana'ewa	Place on the Hilo side of Hawai'i Island, famous for *maile* and resistant Hawaiians
Pele	Goddess of the volcano, who may appear as a young or old woman; also the fire of the volcano itself
Pele'aihonua	Pele, the volcano deity, who literally eats the land *('aihonua)*
Pelehonuamea	Another name for Pele, as in "Earth Mother"
pīkake	The Arabian jasmine, introduced to Hawai'i from India; very fragrant small white flowers often used for *lei* and other decoration
Pō Mahina	Night of the full moon, night for lovers
pū	Large triton conch or helmet shell used as a trumpet
pua	Flower
pulu	A glossy yellow wool on the base of tree-fern stalks
Puna	District of Hawai'i Island, famous because it is home to Pele and her sisters
Punalu'u	District on both O'ahu and Hawai'i; on the latter island, famous for black sand beaches
Pūowaina	Hill on O'ahu where the American National Cemetery of the Pacific is located; literally, the hill of sacrifice; also known as Punchbowl
Rarotonga	Island to the far south of Hawai'i, part of the Cook Islands in central Polynesia

taro	Starchy tuber that is the staple of the Hawaiian diet; *kalo* in Hawaiian. Metaphorically, *taro* is the parent of the Hawaiian people.
ti	A woody plant in the lily family with long, bright green or multicolored leaves, used to make *lei* and other adornments
tiare	Tahitian gardenia
'ulu	Breadfruit
wa'a	Canoe
wahine	Woman
wahine u'i	A beautiful woman
wai	Water
Waiāhole	Land division on the windward or Ko'olau side of O'ahu
Wai'anae	Hot, dry district on leeward O'ahu
Waihe'e	District on Maui; also the name of the first elected governor of Hawaiian ancestry after statehood in 1959; name translates as "runny squid water"
Waikīkī	Place in Honolulu, world famous as a tourist destination; literally, spouting water
Waimānalo	District on the windward side of O'ahu, famous for long beaches with fine white sand

ABOUT THE AUTHOR

Haunani-Kay Trask is one of Hawai'i's most recognized Native authors. Essayist, political theorist, and lyric poet, Trask has been a leader in the Native Hawaiian sovereignty movement for the past twenty years. Her previous works include the best-selling collection of essays *From a Native Daughter: Colonialism and Sovereignty in Hawai'i* and a volume of poetry, *Light in the Crevice Never Seen.* Trask coproduced the 1993 award-winning film *Act of War: The Overthrow of the Hawaiian Nation.*

Trask lectures widely in the United States and the Pacific Basin. In 2001 she was part of the Hawai'i delegation to the United Nations World Conference against Racism held in Durban, South Africa.